Little Rhymes

Beverley Randell and Debbie Croft

Rhymes About Monkey, Rabbit and Little Teddy
The Boat Ride	2
The Race	4

Rhymes About Jack and Billy
Playing with Dad	6
Billy Is Hiding	8
The Big Hit	10
New Boots	12

Rhymes About the Toytown Vehicles
The Toytown Tow Truck	14
The Toytown Fire Engine	16

The Boat Ride

One day, Monkey and Rabbit
Went out in a boat for a ride.
They came back to get Little Teddy,
And he sat in the boat
                  by their side.

3

The Race

Little Teddy said to Monkey,
"I will race you if you like.
You go on your skateboard,
And I will ride my bike."

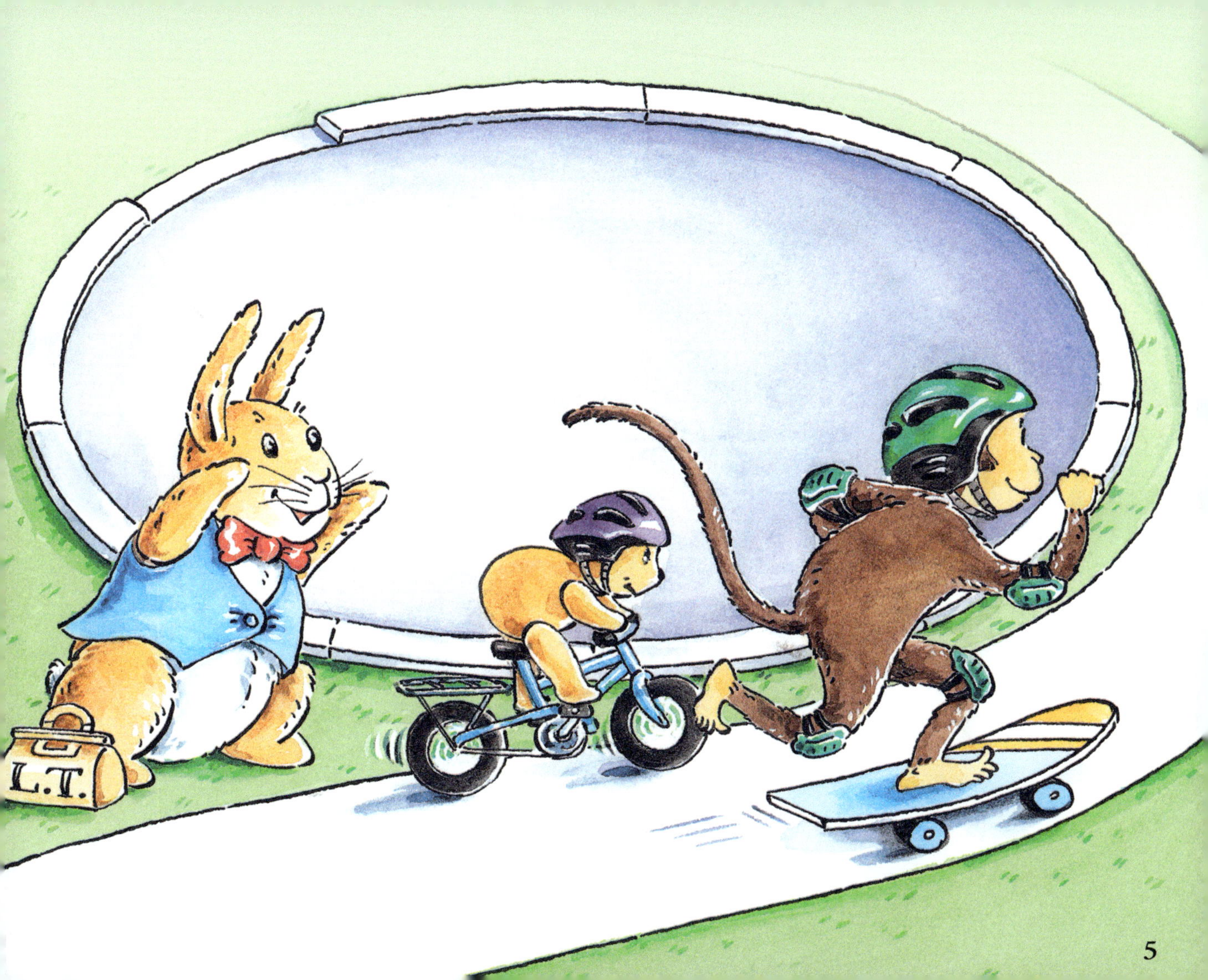
L.T.

Playing with Dad

Jack is riding on his dad,

He sits up on his back.

Billy wants to climb up, too,

Behind his brother Jack.

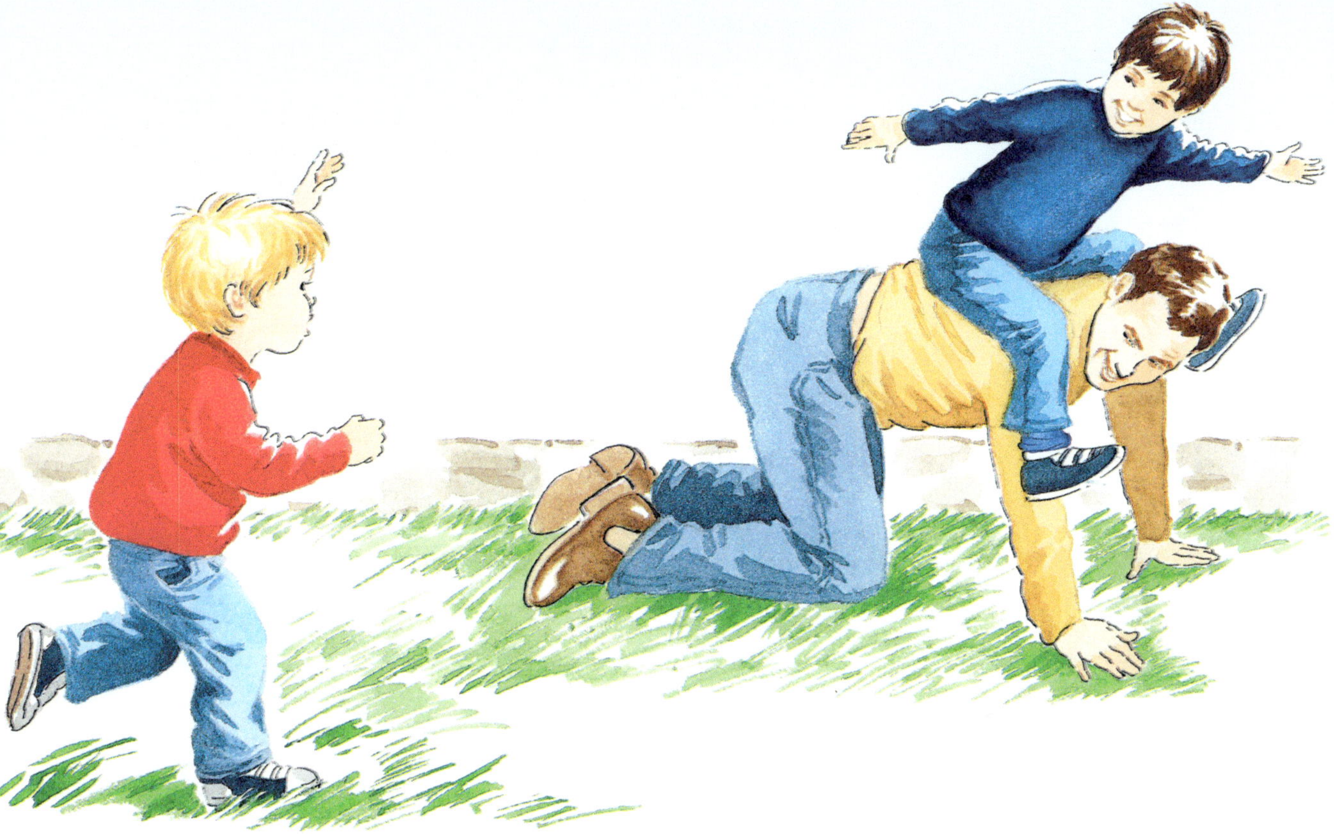

Billy Is Hiding

Is Billy hiding in the chair?

Is Billy hiding by the door?

Is Billy hiding in the bed?

No — he's hiding on the floor.

9

The Big Hit

Billy wants to hit the ball.

Billy says he's not too small.

Here comes the ball.

He hits it hard …

Away it goes across the yard!

11

New Boots

Jack and Billy have new boots.

Billy's boots are red.

Billy loves his new red boots.

He keeps them on ...

                         in bed!

13

The Toytown Tow Truck

"Little yellow tow truck,
Tell me what you do."

"I can tow a heavy bus.
That is what I do."

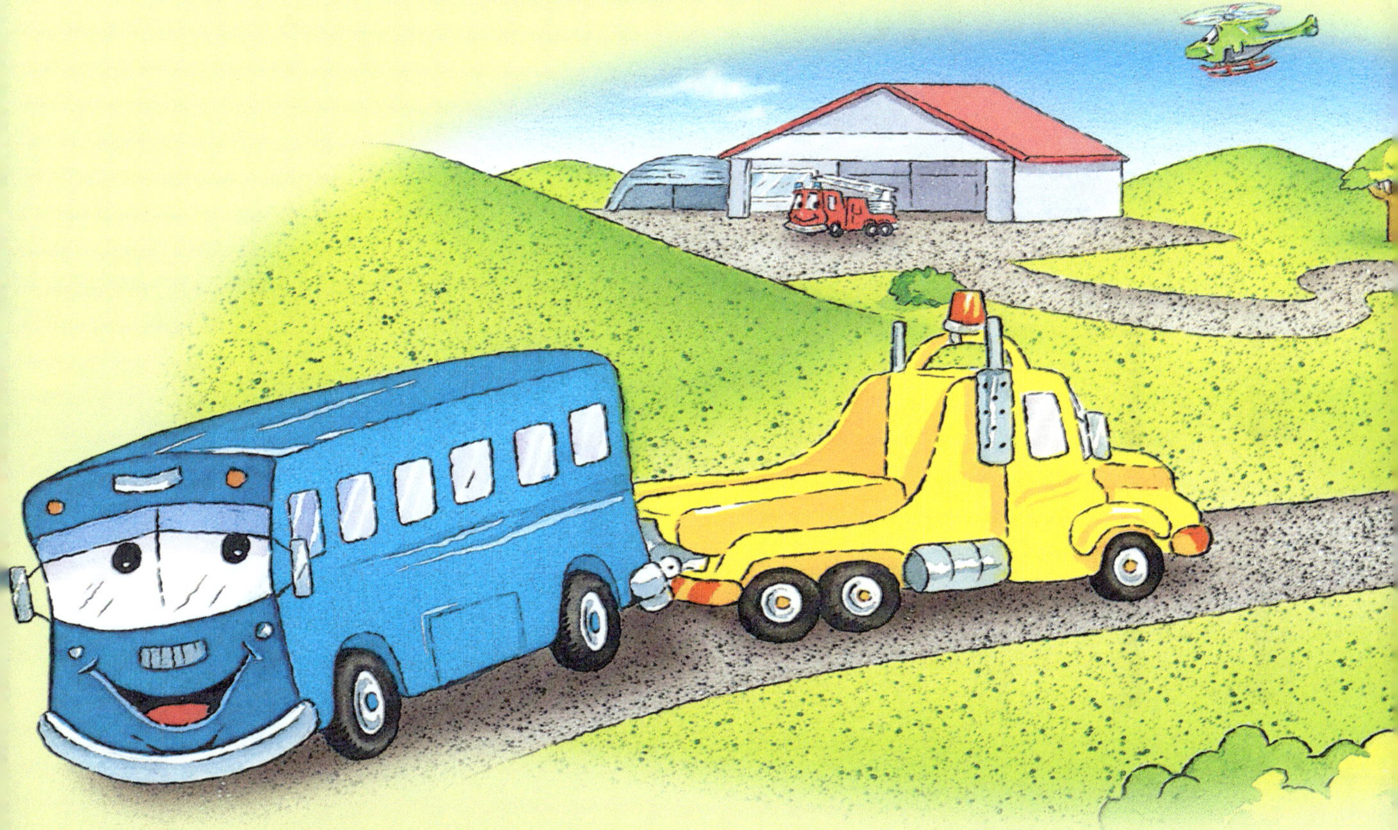

The Toytown Fire Engine

"Little red fire engine,
Tell me what you do."

"I can rescue silly cats.
That is what I do."